The Dirtbag Handbook

Cheap Nomadic Travel in North America

by
Vanessa Runs

Copyright 2017 by Vanessa Runs
First Edition

ISBN: 978-1542754187

Book design: Y42K Publishing Services
http://www.y42k.com/bookproduction.html

For my kitty

Table of Contents

Introduction 7
Chapter 1: Why We Need Dirtbags 14
Chapter 2: How To Downsize 22
Chapter 3: How To Choose Your Travel Buddy .. 25
Chapter 4: How To Camp For Free 29
Chapter 5: What We Eat And Drink 38
Chapter 6: How To Cook 45
Chapter 7: How To Shower 50
Chapter 8: How To Clean 55
Chapter 9: Road-Friendly Travel Apps 58
Chapter 10: How To Travel With Pets 60
Chapter 11: How To Make Social Connections 69
Chapter 12: How To Manage Expenses 72
Chapter 13: How To Earn Money 79
Chapter 14: How To Stay Sustainable 84
Chapter 15: How To Work Offline 88
Chapter 16: How To Give And Accept Hospitality
 91
Chapter 17: The Things I Have Learned 99
Afterword 103
Acknowledgements 106

Stuff your eyes with wonder, live as if you'd drop dead in ten seconds. See the world. It's more fantastic than any dream made or paid for in factories.

- Ray Bradbury

Introduction

I'm lucky.

Every morning I wake up in a beautiful place. Every day, I am excited and stimulated by the tasks at hand. I work hard and vigorously and joyfully. Every afternoon, I venture into the mountains for play and exploration. Every evening, I crawl into a warm bed with a snoozing dog and I am stunned—amazed at how great my life is.

People say my husband and I are living the dream. Not the American dream of working hard and building a comfortable life for our children, but the other one of rambling the planet full-time with few possessions. We live simply and comfortably and contentedly without full-time jobs.

How did we get here?

About Us

Years ago I asked myself one question that changed my life: "What could I do in one year if nothing were holding me back?"

By nothing I meant my own fear of leaping into the unknown, the uncertainty and insanity of leaving my steady job in a failing economy, and the trepidation of traveling to places I had never been before. It took courage to make that first leap, but I have been greatly rewarded since that day.

My husband Shacky and I have been living full-time in a 22-foot Rialta RV since 2012. It has taken us 100,000 miles to criss-cross the continent in almost four years. We have been to both the Pacific and Atlantic coasts. We have seen all the tallest mountains and even climbed some of them. We have wet our toes in each of the Great Lakes.

We travel with a senior dog and a mostly-feral cat I love just as wildly. (Edit: My dear kitty passed away, purring peacefully in my arms as I was writing this book. We shared a beautiful life together and her insufferable stubbornness will live in my heart forever.)

In our first year of travel, Shacky and I were eager tourists, driving every day and covering as many sights and miles as we could, fearing the world would disappear before we had a chance to see it all. In those first 12 months we ran 2,000 miles of trail, drove 30,000 miles of scenic routes, and visited 17 national parks.

The years after that we took on some bigger projects: driving through Alaska one summer, traveling across Canada in the fall, working and living in a homestead all winter, and crewing our friends as they ran across America.

After that, we mellowed out. We grew more picky with our destinations, and spent more time at them. Summer in Colorado. Fall in the Grand Canyon. Winter in Arizona. We bought items that, for us, implied some level of more permanent camping: a small table and bird feeders. We watched the sun rise and set in the same place more than two days in a row. We gave out GPS coordinates so our friends could visit.

Today we savor a travel pace that shifts with the seasons and soothes my soul. The days are long and stunning and snow-capped. I feel a complete freedom to pursue any idea that intrigues me. We have learned to live contentedly and comfortably without full-time employment. I simply cannot imagine a more fulfilling life for myself.

What is a Dirtbag?

A dirtbag is anyone who is drawn to this nomadic existence. It's someone who loves being outdoors, who is a little weird and unconventional by society's narrow standards, and who thinks outside the cubicle.

If you're reading this with interest, I already consider you my fellow dirtbag. Don't be offended — the word dirtbag is shedding its previous connotations of a lazy hobo eager to take advantage of your good will. Generations of dirtbag ambassadors are now rising up and claiming the title as eager and engaged individuals who value time over money, experience over status, and environment over merchandise. Dirtbag doesn't mean homeless, or even unemployed. Homelessness is not a choice. Dirtbag life is.

Dirtbagging can appeal to a wide variety of personality types. However, I have observed that the most successful and the most satisfied low-income travelers share some basic qualities. You may have the heart of a true dirtbag if you are:

Open-minded and Understanding

You often find yourself in situations outside of your comfort zone, facing experiences that you are not used to. You meet people who seem to be polar opposites of you, people whose views and lifestyles you don't agree with, even people who embrace beliefs that make you rage internally.

You find a way to grow in grace and compassion. You remain open-minded and find points of commonality with anyone. You view these as learning opportunities. You seek to understand people who think and live differently than you do. You've come to value human life regardless of creed, race, belief, or political stand.

Curious and Willing

When you have the opportunity to do things that

make you feel scared or nervous, you choose to seize them regardless of your terror. You know you will be better for it because the habit of facing your fears has followed you through life. You are curious about life and people. You are constantly moving and evolving and learning.

Independent and Content

You are comfortable with down time. Your free time is filled with quiet contemplation and observation, independently exploring your own mind. You are comfortable in solitude. You find refuge in your stories and ideas. You are highly creative and, left to your own devices, never bored. You only need a small handful of close friends to feel socially fulfilled. You are less go-go-go and more breathe-breathe-breathe.

Self-monitoring and Self-knowlegeable

You understand your own strengths and weaknesses. You tend to focus on what you do best and you trust your intuition. When presented with a wide variety of seemingly endless choices, you know almost instantly which ones you want to pursue.

Ambitious and Internally Motivated

You appreciate accountability, but you don't need it to be productive. You tend to set goals and just run with them. When a project interests you, are are fiercely loyal to it and you're not afraid to work day and night to make your vision a reality. You don't like people looking over your shoulder or micro managing you. You are very proud of what you have accomplished in life so far.

What to Expect from This Book

The purpose of this book is to give you the confidence and empowerment to take up the dirtbag lifestyle, if it calls to you. I do this by walking you through the details of how and why and where we live, as well as how we can afford it. You will be able to use our experiences to enhance and create your own journey.

In four years, we have not paid for any lodging or camping or amenities. No mortgage, no car payments, no utilities. Our biggest expenses are food and gas, and we exist comfortably on 1,500/month. These days we are spending more and more time off the grid. At any point, you can follow our travels as they happen at vanessaruns.com.

This book is not meant to convince people to adopt our lifestyle. I've never met a dirtbag that needed to be convinced to do some dirtbagging. Instead, I've written the book I wish I had read before I hit the road. It contains all the shortcuts and loopholes it took me four years to figure out. My message is about empowering people to follow their particular brand of dreams, regardless of how unlikely they seem. I hope this book will be a valuable guide on your own journey of adventure and discovery.

In these pages you will learn:
- How much money we make, how we make it, and where we spend it
- Where and how to find free camping across North America
- How we obtain food and how we store it
- What we do with our garbage and sewage
- Dirtbag hygiene and how come we're so damn handsome
- Life lessons we've learned on the road
- How to travel full-time with entitled pets
- How we engage with society while living primarily off-grid

Ultimately, this book is about taking charge of your own life. It's about following your intuition and structuring a life that is perfectly suited to your needs and interests. I hope to guide you through the process, but the journey is ultimately yours. Don't be afraid to get your hands dirty. Try new things. Break some rules. Change your mind. Create. Learn. Grow. Your adventure awaits.

Chapter 1: Why We Need Dirtbags

"All the 'free' things you enjoy are due to others working for them… You are a freeloader that survives because society has enough slack to support a small number of people who don't produce anything. You're not living; you're surviving in spite of the universe being generally set against you."
– comment left on my blog in 2013

Dirtbag life is generally accepted for 20-somethings eager to see the world before they "settle down" with a real job and a real family. But what if you're pushing 30 or 40 or 50 and still want to live this way? Suddenly society views your choice as a sign of something unsettling or immature.

My husband and I are sometimes called freeloaders. We are accused of contributing nothing to society, or worse—burdening it. Dirtbags have a reputation of being takers, not givers.

Before I get into the details of how we live, I need to clarify and validate this lifestyle. Dirtbag life is not a misguided attempt to flee responsibility. It is a respectable and fulfilling choice. As much as we need doctors and construction workers—we need dirtbags.

Here's why:

1. Dirtbags teach us to respect our resources and show us how it is possible to live well with less.

Can you brush your teeth with two sips of water? Can you shower without a shower stall? What if all the water you had access to was the amount you could carry on your back? What if all the trash you could make was limited to what you could hike with? What if the only light you had after dark was the moon?

As a dirtbag, I have learned to use less water and produce less garbage. I rely on solar power. I am resourceful enough to fix things when they break instead of throwing them away or buying new things. Many dirtbags live this way. It's not a weekend camping trip; it's just life. Most importantly—it's not that hard.

Society tends to buy into extremes: either we live large or live in a cave with nothing. Dirtbags know there is a sweet middle ground and we walk it daily. We can drastically reduce our footprint on this planet yet still function in a civilized society.

2. Dirtbags change the way we think and view the world.

Once we have met our basic needs of food, shelter, and security, many of us feel pressured to over-develop those amenities: a bigger house, a nicer car, giving our kids everything they could possibly desire and not just what they need. To achieve this, we sacrifice the higher levels of humanity: friendships, self-esteem, and the freedom to slow down.

Dirtbags flip those priorities upside down. We embrace the bare minimum when it comes to food and shelter in exchange for the higher opportunities of self-actualization. We have the freedom to immerse ourselves into areas that the rest of society has little time for: volunteering, extensive travel, spiritually fulfilling year-long projects with little to no financial return, and time-consuming works of art.

We learn from dirtbags that more money does not equal more freedom and that a full-time, year-round, steady paycheck is not necessary to eat and sleep and live in contentment and comfort.

3. Dirtbags fight stereotypes by migrating different world views across regional lines.

Dirtbags infuse the world with people who can relate to different perspectives. We carry the message that there is more than one way to do things and we refute stereotypes wherever we travel. Every community seeks to bond over common ideas, but once in a while you need a dirtbag to shake things up in places where everyone thinks the same, earns the same, and votes the same.

We need dirtbags to remind us that our biases do

not apply to every inch of this planet. We also need dirtbags to carry our stories off to places where our habits are considered strange.

4. Dirtbags expose us to a full spectrum of human experiences that feed our sense of humanity.

Back when I had a "real" job and a "real" home, it was easy for me to disconnect. Routine set in, and my emotions were dulled. There was nothing new or exciting, and there was nothing to make me angry or annoyed. I had tweaked my world for maximum comfort and slipped into a state of complete moderation.

Now I exist in a world where anything can happen at any time, deep in the margins of society. I often see, hear, and feel those who have no voice, no words, and no education. This has changed the way I feel about the universe and my role on this planet.

5. Dirtbags help us see exercise and movement as a way of life, not an activity we need to schedule.

In my pre-dirtbag days, I would log all my exercise on a site called Dailymile. At the end of the week, it would give me a grand total and tell me I was awesome. After we hit the road, logging workouts became more complicated. Without a GPS surgically attached to my wrist, I had no idea how far I had moved. I no longer went out to do a workout. I just went out to play or work. This healthy concept of movement was a welcome change for me.

6. Dirtbags connect us to themselves and each other.

Dirtbags are more trusting of strangers than your average person, probably because they spend a larger portion of their time talking to them. They discover that strangers (and humans in general) are inherently good, hospitable, and eager to help. As a result, dirtbags serve as society's connectors.

They will:
- connect people with similar interests to each other
- connect people with resources to people in need
- connect strangers in close proximity
- connect with Facebook friends face-to-face

Dirtbags not only make frequent connections, but also improve the quality of those connections. They have the time to listen and understand the people they meet. Their attentions are focused on the stories and experiences of others.

7. Dirtbags bring us back to our roots of self-sufficiency, trade, and simple survival.

We live in a society full of individuals who are quickly losing the skill and ability to feed themselves. More and more, we are socialized with the idea that if we need something, we must buy it. Many dirtbags know how to be self-sufficient. They work on farms in exchange for room and board. They are also resourceful experts at acquiring the things they need without using money. They barter and trade their services, goods, or skills. No matter how industrialized we become, these survival skills are highly valuable.

8. Dirtbags feed our inherent sense of curiosity, wonder, and adventure; they give us permission to follow our own senseless dreams.

In a society that demands a purpose and a rational explanation for any expenditure of energy, dirtbags represent travel, movement, and adventure as worthwhile pursuits in themselves. Theirs are the adventures that inspire legends. This is where original ideas are born and lives are changed. The destination is senseless and the journey is the point.

The benefits of living vicariously through your local dirtbag are also abundant. Not all of us will quit our jobs and travel the world, but many of us have our own brands of irrational dreams that we've muted because of society's expectations. Sometimes it takes a dirtbag to come along and give us a little courage to pursue them.

9. Dirtbags give us permission to love ourselves.

There are currently dirtbag spirits out there,

chained to their cubicles, because they are convinced that travel would be selfish. Travel is not selfish. Dirtbag travel can never be selfish, because for every benefit you receive, you give away everything—your entire heart, your mind, strength, and life—to forever change the people you meet and quietly improve the places you visit.

The Drawbacks of Dirtbag Life

This lifestyle is not for everyone. You may find it frustrating if:

- You need routine and control over the daily details of your life.
- You are deeply attached to items of sentimental value.
- You have a large family you need to be close to.
- You love full-time access to amenities and creature comforts.
- You love and care for large animals.
- You are a passionate collector of large physical objects.
- You are passionate about a hobby that takes up a lot of space.
- You love to organize and host big communal gatherings.
- You need consistency in your athletic training.
- You want your children to grow up like their

peers.
- You need roots and permanency.
- You dislike exposure to the outdoors.
- You need to meet regularly with others.

Understanding and honoring yourself as well as your needs are a good idea regardless of lifestyle. Don't become a dirtbag because it's trendy and all your friends are doing it. Do it because it feeds your soul and compliments who you already are.

Chapter 2: How To Downsize

Our possessions can take up an obscene amount of energy, time, and money. The act of purging your belongings and simplifying your life is a euphoric experience that leaves you feeling weightless and free. Minimizing and simplifying your life is a process, and a never-ending one at that. I can't tell you exactly how many possessions you should own because the goal isn't to get rid of everything. The goal is to surround yourself with only those things that bring you joy and improve your life.

1. Be selective with what you sell.

Don't sweat the small stuff. It is often not worth making and managing a Craigslist ad for every object. Selling your possessions takes more time and energy than most people realize. Sometimes the ease of donating or giving away your stuff is worth the loss of a few dollars in sales.

2. Consider donating as much as possible.

Libraries are great to keep in mind for unused books or CDs/DVDs. Often charities will come by and pick up furniture. You'll be saving yourself the headache of trying to close a sale.

The Dirtbag Handbook

3. Digitize your life.

Photos and home movies are easy to store online. You can also digitize sentimental paperwork like letters or journals. They don't take up any space and you will likely access them more often. You can store important paperwork as PDFs and opt for paperless options when it comes to bills and financial statements.

4. Beware of the storage trap.

The cost and stress of storage is usually not worth the value of the items that people store. Sometimes it's cheaper to just rent or borrow any gear you will use seasonally. Even a small space will set you back at least $200/month. If you're on the road for four years like us, that's almost $10,000 in storage fees. None of my possessions are worth that much. Are yours?

5. Purge yearly.

Once or twice a year, I go through everything in the RV and ditch the things we haven't used in the past 12 months. You can also use the 90/90 rule: Have you used it in the last 90 days or will you use it in the next 90 days? If not, you don't need it.

6. Refuse to accumulate.

Inevitably, new objects will come into your life. If you know right away that you won't use them, refuse if possible. For us, this mostly happens with the free swag at races. If there's a clothing item or a product that I know for sure I won't use, I don't accept it. In the past, we have quietly handed back our race t-shirts and finisher medals. We rarely value the merchandise, but we treasure the experience.

Although this process can be difficult and time consuming the first time around, it feels like a deep soul cleanse. A weight is lifted off your shoulders you didn't even know was there.

Sometimes the things we own can become our chains. They bind us to one space, to one room, to one idea. Letting things go forces a mind cleanse. Suddenly, we have more options. We can see ourselves in a different perspective. We can change.

Chapter 3: How To Choose Your Travel Buddy

> *Life has taught us that love does not consist in gazing at each other but in looking outward together in the same direction.*
> *- Antoine de Saint-Exupery*

I attribute the peace in my relationship with Shacky to simple living combined with compatibility. Both of us have a similar temperament: laid-back, calm, and low maintenance. We both enjoy this lifestyle and we don't fight the typical stressors of other couples: debt, work, time management, children.

That said, things like hunger and bad weather can make us both grumpy. Despite our discomforts, we tend to be angry at our circumstances or other people (bad drivers, etc) rather than each other. Many of our challenges involve working as a team (researching places to go, organizing travel details, navigating new terrain). This has produced an "us against the world" mindset that motivates us to cooperate and compromise.

I read a great quote from Gunter Holtorf, a 75-year-old world traveler who has driven his car (and lived in it) for more than 820,000 kilometers all over the world. He traveled with his wife until she passed away. He writes:

"When you live in a car for nearly 20 years, it's not a normal situation of a couple living in a home. Living in the car, and doing all that travel over all those years is like living as Siamese twins. When you travel like that, you can't say, 'I'm going to go read a book in the garden.' You are stuck together, 24 hours a day. The only splits would be if one of us went shopping, or if you go behind a tree to use a toilet. You are bound to be together."

1. Make sure he doesn't mind sharing your leg hole.

There's a social media meme going around where mothers take a picture of their kids with a caption of why they were crying. There was this one poor boy who found himself sitting in a grocery store cart, sharing the double toddler seat with what appeared to be his sister. She was just chilling out, sucking her pacifier, while he was having a complete meltdown. The caption: "He didn't want to share his leghole."

There are a thousand and one ways you must share a leghole with your dirtbag companion. In bed, in bathrooms, in living space. Make it a leg you enjoy.

2. Don't mind the poop.

With a living space as small as ours, expect to poop in close proximity of each other. It doesn't matter how long you've been in a relationship — you're either comfortable with poops or you're not. If you're not, things are about to get weird for you.

3. Like similar likes.

If one of you is passionate about backcountry trail running and other one loves deep sea ice fishing, you may be in for a minor conflict. Fortunately, there are many things that go together. When Shacky took up fly fishing, I had no interest in it. While he fished, I went trail running or hiking.

4. Get comfortable with farts.

Not currently comfortable with farts? You need to GET comfortable with farts because there's going to be a lot and they're going to be heading in your general direction. Instead of freaking out, learn to have fun with it. Fart baseball is a game our friend Patrick Sweeney taught us. Here are the general rules:

Recommended players: 2-8

Object of the game: To get to home plate for the most number of points.

When a batter farts, they are on first base. Each consecutive fart advances the player a base. If the player farts 4 times in a row then they score a point.

However, if another player in the game farts while someone is on base, then the player on base must start all over; he's been tagged out. The player who has just farted is then on first base. Farts must be audible, and another fart baseball player must be present to witness the base hit. The most number of runs wins.

Within this universe, the rules can become as complex and intricate as you desire. Most will agree that if you poop yourself, that's an automatic home run. If you can make your opponent smell your fart without hearing it, that's a stolen base. Games can go on for weeks.

5. Take a chance.

Sometimes you just know. You have a feeling or intuition about someone and you know you'll get along well. That's how it was for Shacky and I. We were a fairly new couple when we decided to travel together, but it was the best decision we ever made. When I asked Shacky what his tips were for choosing the right travel partner, he said, "Fuck, I dunno."

Chapter 4: How To Camp For Free

Our preferred style of camping is commonly known as boondocking or dry camping. Additionally, we spend most of our time off-the-grid.

Boondocking means camping without hooking into sewage, power, or water. Instead, we rely on solar panels. We fill and carry our own water jugs, and we utilize free public sewage dumps. We carry our own built-in propane, which we use in combination with campfires for both cooking and heat. We do not use a generator. We do not use a fridge.

Off-the-grid means we are rarely connected to a phone or wifi or data. My internet access is limited to chore days when we head into town. This is usually my only opportunity to send email or scroll social media. I am online for approximately one hour every ten days. I sometimes auto-schedule one social media post per week, but I am never online when the posts go live. For two years, we travelled without a cell phone. Now we carry one for emergencies.

We are a self-sufficient and self-contained unit, capable of parking and living anywhere.

Remember, each of these details have been choices for us based on the things we value (or don't value).

None of these simplicities have felt like sacrifices to us. In fact, we are currently making plans to downgrade. As it is, we still feel we have too much.

What is our Camp Life Like?

When we first started traveling, we were eager to see everything. We drove everyday, usually one to three hours, and explored many major national parks. We also tackled most of the well-known physical challenges among our athletic endurance friends, like summiting Mount Whitney and completing 100-mile foot races. We moved quickly and didn't stay anywhere very long.

Over the years we have transitioned into a slower version of travel. I want to travel deeply now, not just widely. I want to take the time to learn about each place we call home and meet up with the locals. We pick one area per season and explore it thoroughly. One year it was winter in Arizona, spring in the Adirondaks, summer in Colorado, and fall at the Grand Canyon.

We park in one spot for one to two weeks, then drive into the nearest town for one day of chores. These chores can include laundry, grocery shopping, sewage dumps, vet visits, wifi, water refills, library visits, etc. Fully stocked, we head back out to camp for another one to two weeks. Repeat.

A Word About Solar Panels

Our current camping freedom would not be possible without solar power. The solar panels we installed on our roof were our first and our most valuable upgrade.

Our solar panels were installed by Mike in Slab City. He runs a company called SunWorks. Because he lives in the middle of the desert and doesn't advertise, he offers amazing deals. He did the work well, quickly, and incredibly cheap. Slab City is an off-the-grid community of squatters near the Salton Sea. It has the feel of a homeless camp, but it is also a draw for hippies and artists. We have spent many days in this amazing place.

I use solar to charge my laptop, my iPod, and a Kindle. My husband Shacky has his own laptop. We never use appliances (no microwave, blender, toaster, coffee maker, etc). We rarely run out of power.

For more information on solar panels for travelers, I recommend this article on Cheap RV Living: http://www.cheaprvliving.com/blog/frequently-asked-questions-about-solar/

It covers most of the FAQs we get as well as extra advice and tips. You'll read about how and where to purchase solar panels, as well as assessing your needs and getting set up. You'll also find a wider variety of links and resources. I can't rave enough about our solar panels.

Where We Camp for Free

BLM Public Lands

The Bureau of Land Management (BLM) is an agency within the USA that administers more than 247.3 million acres of public lands. They allow camping for two weeks to one month at a time. This is our primary preference. There are no amenities, but there is a lot of space, trail access, and we are often completely alone. Seclusion, solitude, and silence are the campground qualities I most highly value.

LTVA Spots

This stands for long-term camping. These are spots where, for a small fee, you can park semi-permanently for half the year or months at a time. Some popular locations include Holtville and Quartzite in Arizona. These are particularly popular with the snowbirds. Essentially, these become small communities with the same people returning year after year and bonding with one another. Many offer a garbage dump and a sewage dump, though generally no hookups for water or power or sewage. We have stayed very close to these locations, just outside the fee boundaries.

American National Parks

An America the Beautiful pass will allow you to

enter federal land, and many parks also offer camping. The less popular parks are easier to stay in long-term while the major ones (like Grand Canyon) have more limited options. We pay $80 for an annual American pass and it pays itself off within a month. There is an equivalent access pass in Canada. And in Canada, dogs are allowed in the national parks.

Closed Campgrounds

After Labor Day, many public campgrounds begin shutting down. This means the water shuts down, the bathrooms close, and the garbage dumps are locked. However, if you are dry camping like we do and don't need any of those conveniences, you can almost always have the entire campground to yourself, for free. Please be respectful and leave no trace.

State Parks

Several states offer state park passes that allow you to camp on these lands for extended periods of time. Check online for your local state park information, as they all vary.

Outdoor Stores

Several outdoor establishments like REI, Mountain Equipment Co-op, Bass Pro Shop, bike shops, and others often allow urban camping in their parking lots. Make sure you go inside and ask. If they don't formally allow camping, many of these places will still give you permission to park overnight. This goes for any company with an appealing parking lot. We have asked for permission at gas stations, restaurants (after eating there), and retail stores. We have only been refused once in four years.

Friends' Driveways

In major cities that ban street parking and frown on the act of sleeping in your vehicle, our only real option (if we don't want to pay camping fees) is to crash in the driveways of our friends. Fortunately, our travels have introduced us to new friends all over the country and we are frequently sent open invitations to drop by anytime. When we do, we spend the day enjoying food and drink and catching up with old friends. Many offer us a bed indoors, but I prefer the RV.

Walmart

Most Walmarts allow free overnight camping in their parking lots. However, this is my least favorite place to stay and our absolutely last resort. We use Walmarts when we are making a long drive to a specific destination and don't have much time for sidetracking. We will drive for the majority of the day, crash at a Walmart, and leave as soon as we wake up.

The things I hate about Walmarts are: lights, noise

and company. I have trouble sleeping under fluorescent lights but if we park to avoid them, we usually end up in unsavory and/or illegal company. It seems that we are either being approached for drugs or kept up all night with constant generator noise.

We locate most of our camping spots on freecampsites.net, but in the first year we experimented with phone apps. Here are some of the apps we have used successfully locate a place to spend the night:
- Free RV Campgrounds
- RV Parky
- Couchsurfing
- AllTrails

A Note on Weather

When you're living indoors, it's easy to become disconnected from the elements. That's not the case for the full-time dirtbag.

Early on in our travels we thought it would be a great idea to spend the winter living and working at a friend's homestead in rural Pennsylvania. Although our time there was epic and I don't regret the memories we made, the RV and the animals all suffered from one of the harshest winters Pennsylvania had seen to date.

We also didn't have the mobility we were used to. Our tires became completely frozen into blocks of ice and by the time April rolled around, the ice still hadn't melted. We were stranded. In our final days at the farm, I was taking an ice pick to those tires every day, desperately trying to dig an escape. We accumulated moisture in the RV which led to spots of mold and destroyed internal electrical connections. It was incredibly expensive to fix. We spent an unexpected amount of time and an exorbitant amount of money due to our poor decision of camping in the cold.

Another year we spent several weeks in Portland, Oregon where it rained seemingly day and night. Since we rely on solar panels for power, we would be out of power by 10 am every day. This also limited our outdoor time, particularly with the dog. During this time, we developed a leak on the roof of the RV we have still not been able to find. Over time, this began causing water damage on the roof. These areas were beautiful and although we had some great days there, they were ultimately not worth the rain.

One year we made the mistake of venturing into Phoenix, AZ in the summer to face off with a heat so excruciating we were forced to keep driving so the A/C would run. Neither the dog or the cat could set foot outside, and I could barely stand ten minutes. If it had just been Shacky and I, we would have spent the day in a library or a public place with air conditioning. But we couldn't leave the animals in a hot car without A/C. So we drove and drove and never made that mistake again.

All of this could have been avoided if we had taken the weather more seriously. These days we keep a closer eye on weather and we don't take chances. We are influenced by the elements every day.

Chapter 5: What We Eat And Drink

This section serves up a glimpse of which foods travel well and fit our best version of a healthy and empathic diet. I highly value eating compassionately. This means choosing foods with the least possible impact on the environment, with minimal or no packaging, and buying only what is absolutely necessary so there is no waste. It also means eating mindfully with gratitude for all the souls that contributed to our meal.

Over the years Shacky and I have experimented with a variety of diets, including vegan, paleo, and low-carb. We've done well on several of them, but ultimately could not sustain any one diet during our entire traverse across North America. Access and availability were huge issues.

We no longer follow a specific diet, but rather try to eat as locally as possible wherever we are. We buy our staples in bulk and since we don't own a fridge or microwave, these are mostly dry goods. We cook once or twice a day.

Here is an overview of some of our staple foods:

Beans and Rice

Beans are an awesome compliment to the dirtbag diet. We buy our beans in bulk, then soak and cook them, usually with rice. Pinto and black beans are a favorite. Shacky makes a great bean stew with veggies. We also make bean wraps with tortillas.

Couscous

This is my favorite grain because it's so quick to prepare. I normally boil water in my JetBoil, add it to some dry couscous, and in minutes I have a grain I can use as a base to host my eggs or sardines or veggies. Sometimes I eat it like grits with just butter and salt. Other times I'll make it into an oatmeal with peanut butter and nuts.

Eggs

Eggs are probably the healthiest form of protein you can eat, and one of the easiest to consume on the road in hard boiled form. Both the animals are egg fans too. We normally have some raw eggs for the animals and for cooking breakfast, plus hardboiled eggs we can throw into soups and salads, or just pop in our mouths raw.

Pickled Vegetables

These don't spoil as quickly as the fresh versions and are usually nutritionally sound. We eat a variety of vegetables in pickled form including but not limited to:

beets, asparagus, olives, and mushrooms. Pickled foods are much easier to store and we usually re-use the pickling juice for things like boiled eggs or even raw veggies that we'd like to preserve a little longer.

Canned Sardines and Other Fish

Sardines are a great source of nutrients and they're easy to eat as a snack. They are also one of the most sustainable canned fish you can buy. I normally add a can of sardines to any salad or soup I prepare (my two favorite meals), or just eat them straight out of the can. We normally buy canned sardines in bulk from Costco. They don't take up a lot of room and they last a long time. In the spring and summer, Shacky fishes for most of our protein. We eat a lot of freshly caught trout.

Carrots and Celery

These two vegetables require less refrigeration and work perfectly with our soups and stews. Most fresh veggies are tricky to store for us, so these are the main two we consume fresh.

Potatoes

You can't beat a good potato baked slowly over a campfire, then covered in butter and hot sauce. Potatoes are delicious and extremely easy to prepare. They are also incredibly versatile and cheap, cheap, cheap. We eat them almost daily.

Nuts

Normally these are snacks in the evening, or a compliment to a morning oatmeal. Even the dog loves almonds and cashews. We buy our nuts in bulk, then mix and repackage them in reusable containers. Anytime we are near a Sprouts, which isn't often, we splurge for their salt and vinegar almonds — to die for!

Coconut Oil

This keeps really well and it's full of nutrition. We use it to cook everything from omelets to pancakes.

Fermented Foods

The benefit of these, besides being super healthy, is that they don't go bad as quickly and usually don't require refrigeration until you've opened them. Tempeh is a favorite. It's easy to add to salads or tacos or even soup, and we both like the flavor. Sauerkraut, kambucha and kimchi are also winners.

Dark Chocolate

It's a rare day when we don't have a tiny bit of dark chocolate squirreled away somewhere. After dinner Shacky and I like to settle into bed with some movies and two small pieces of dark chocolate.

Dolmas

Dolmas are grape leaves stuffed with rice and spices. They are high in calories, making them an ideal mid-hike snack.

Sauces

We travel with many different kinds of hot sauces, plus lime juice. We are huge sauce eaters. Shacky is a hardcore hot sauce lover and I like more of a medium heat. We both put hot sauce on everything, including salad.

Wine

Shacky says that with a little bit of boxed wine, we can go anywhere and survive any adventure. A truer truth was never spoken. To further conserve space, we often remove the wine from its box and only use the bag. When we drink with friends, we will generally splurge for higher quality wine, but don't feel it's necessary on a daily basis.

Water

At full capacity, we carry 8 gallons of potable water with us. This can last us anywhere from a week to two weeks, depending on fluctuating weather and hydration needs. The RV itself has a reservoir tank that we use for washing dishes and other non-potable chores. We don't have any running water, but we have two solar showers we hang from trees that function as pseudo-taps.

From brushing our teeth to grooming, we conserve

water in everything we do. The longer we can make our water last, the longer we can hold off going into town for a refill. When our water runs out, we can refill our bottles at:
- A local creek or stream
- A friend's house
- A local park
- Water fountains
- A local campground
- Most sewage dump stations

Many public water sources tend to shut down in the winter, sometimes leaving us with a huge challenge and a difficult search. Water is life. We don't waste a drop of it and we never ever take it for granted.

How much do we spend on food?

We generally spend around $1,200/month on groceries during the winter, including alcohol. In the spring and summer when Shacky can fish, it can get as low as $500-800/month. We don't currently make financial sacrifices around food and drink... and we both drink. We rarely eat out, but that's because most restaurants aren't dog-friendly.

Our highest expense each month is usually food. I feel we can bring this cost down further by implementing some sort of trapping, hunting, foraging,

Vanessa Runs

drying, brewing and/or gardening. I would like to depend more on the land and less on grocery stores in the coming years. This is a challenge and goal for me.

Chapter 6: How To Cook

We cook in the RV with propane. We have a tiny gas stove with two burners on top of what also doubles as our only table, and we use it frequently. On our tiny stove, we make mostly stews and soups and omelets. Shacky is the cook in the family.

Some truck stops offer propane refills, and so do many U-Hauls. Twenty dollars will fill the entire thing if it's bone dry, and that will usually last us at least a month, and sometimes three if we're not running the heater.

We don't use any camping-specific cooking gear as they are normally expensive. We use the regular supplies you'd find in any home, just way less of them. Washing dishes is still a chore, but it only lasts about three seconds. We carry:

- 1 pot
- 1 pan
- 1 Dutch oven
- 1 percolator
- 1 spatula
- 1 big spoon
- 1 can opener
- 1 cutting board

- 1 cooler
- 1 large knife
- 1 small knife
- 1 pair of scissors
- 1 wine bottle opener
- 1 beer bottle opener
- 2 coffee mugs
- 2 wine cups
- 4 bowls
- 4 plates
- 4 spoons
- 4 forks

A Day in the Life of my Stomach

I wake up anytime between 5 - 8 a.m., according to the sun and my level of slothfulness. The sun peeking through the blinds this morning tells me it's time to wake up and be awesome again. Alas, Shacky has beaten me awake and is already grinding coffee beans.

After a couple of years of relying on instant coffee, I had hope for a better life and so we purchased a percolator. Today I drink my coffee in bed next to my hubby with the dog at my feet, still snoring her senior snore and twitching occasionally against my right foot.

I'm a slow drinker, but I power through and methodically make my way through two cups before I have to get up and use the bathroom. At some point during this time or shortly afterwards, Shacky is cooking breakfast. Usually it's eggs or omelets with bacon and potatoes, but sometimes it's pancakes or French toast. If I can't get Shacky to cook for me, I'll opt for a quick oatmeal or cereal.

Breakfast is really brunch and lunch comes pretty late. By around 2 - 3 p.m. I'm starting to feel hungry again. Usually by this time we've done some sort of physical activity: a hike, a bike ride, a run, or some kettle bell torture.

Lunch is very frequently a soup or stew. If there are any fresh greens around, I'll have a large salad. Shacky might whip up some rice and beans and we'll make burritos. I'm definitely a soup and stew kind of girl. If I had my own way, I'd eat most of my meals with a spoon.

Dinner is generally pretty light since we go to bed early. We'll whip up another salad (any greens or fresh veggies get used immediately since we don't have a good way of storing them) or we'll pick through some leftovers. Add generous servings of wine and you've got yourself a pretty awesome evening. My favorite evening junk foods are popcorn and cereal. I limit myself on cereal since milk is hard to store, but not popcorn.

Food as Currency

We often work for food. In fact, food is way more valuable to us than money. Not only does it save us the gas of a long drive to find a grocery store (most of our campgrounds are quite secluded), but it is something we can always use immediately. Food that is shared is full of communal kindness and love, and that's important to me.

Sometimes we work at a farm in exchange for food. Other times we volunteer at a race or an endurance event that lets us take the leftovers that would have otherwise ended up in the landfill (extra fruit, avocado, soups, salt, etc). If you can figure out some sort of arrangement where you are getting food that would have otherwise been wasted, a heartfelt fist-bump to you. Wasting food is the greatest sin any dirtbag can commit.

Most Memorable Meals

In our second year of travel we drove slowly up the west coast and sampled every local food that caught our interest. I'm a sucker for seafood and on the Oregon coast, I had some of the best meals of my life.

My best meal by far was the clam chowder at Pacific Oyster, a hole-in-the-wall spot. It was the day before my birthday and Shacky chose the restaurant. We also did oyster shots there (my first time!) and they went down so smooth. The chowder made me want to hug someone and then go to sleep.

The strangest drink I ever had was the Wasabi Ginger Ale at Fort George Brewery in Astoria, Oregon. It was really biting and strangely pleasant. It felt like a campfire in your mouth. Shacky loved it. I liked it, but then the taste started building up and it was too much wasabi for me by the end.

The best desert award goes to the Tillamook Cheese Factory Ice Cream, literally any flavor. An extremely close second goes to the Rogue Creamery Blue Cheese Popcorn.

Make no mistake: food is love, mijitos. Take only what you need and share everything you have.

Chapter 7: How To Shower

Some of my favorite dirtbag jokes are personal hygiene jokes. Dirty fingernails are a badge of honor: proof that we touch the earth. The more boring reality is that we're not actually that dirty, and we don't smell any worse than the average homeowner.

In 2016, I only took five traditional showers, but that doesn't mean I don't clean my body. It just means I groom with very little or no running water, and no hot water. This may sound uncomfortable, but it has never been an issue for me. When I was a child I learned to clean my body with only one bucket of lukewarm water. Now I've narrowed that down to one water bottle. These days, I don't value hot showers enough to come out of the woods with any regularity.

The boring secret key to my method is actually constant hygiene. Most people shower once a day, and that's it. I hardly shower, but I constantly monitor my body in other ways. I rinse off my feet, face, and scalp after a dry and dusty run. If I'm feeling humid and sticky, I will wet a washcloth and wipe my body down. I never sit and fester in my own filth yearning for the next shower, but rather take the time to do what I need immediately to feel comfortable. I've been known to "shower" in the middle of a strenuous hike, right out of my hydration pack. It rarely takes more than three minutes.

The amount of water that most people use to shower traditionally is obscene and unnecessary, as are personal hygiene products. I haven't used soap or shampoo in four years and my skin is the healthiest it has ever been: soft to the touch, clear to the eye, and teeming with moisture. There's a difference between clean and squeaky clean. I don't think my skin is supposed to squeak seeing as I'm not made out of plastic.

By the time this chapter is over, you will possess all of my knowledge and skills around low-water hygiene on the road. Here are the ways we stay clean:

Natural Water Showers

My favorite way to shower is in our local creeks or streams or rivers. This is often cold and somewhat public, but also a great pleasure for me. This is strictly a rinse with water and a manual scrub, without the use of soaps or products. I love to sit on a rock half naked and scrub the dirt off my body with my bare fingers. It's a slow, methodical, and meditative practice. I have found my own touch on my own body to be healing. I always walk out with a fresh mind as well as a fresh body.

Solar Showers

When there are no natural water sources to be found, solar showers are the next best thing. We have two separate five-gallon solar showers that we fill up whenever we stop for a water refill. When we're camping, we hang them up on a nearby tree. The nozzle is quick and convenient and preserves more water than a jug. This is another straight rinse, kind of like that short shower you take before jumping in the pool. The water doesn't normally get hot unless we're in California, but I'm fine with room temperature.

Bucket Baths

My father taught me to shower from a bucket as a child and I continued the practice when I lived in Cuba for a month. You simply fill a small bucket with water, then use a rag to clean your extremities first and then your core. Your head and hair are last. Use a cup to pour water over your head, or dunk your head in the bucket if you can. Scrub with your fingers.

Hydration Pack and Water Bottle Showers

I like to hang my hydration pack on a tree in the middle of a hard run, and use the tube as a tiny shower head to soak my scalp and neck and face. It cools me down immediately and washes away any salty sweat. If I have enough water, I'll do my legs and arms as well. If it's hot I will take off my cotton shirt, soak it, then put it back on. It will stay damp against my skin for a luxuriously long time. Don't use all your drinking water for this—only what you can spare. I like to overpack my water so I can "shower" anytime.

Baby Wipes

You don't need to be a baby to use baby wipes. Wet wipes are fast, quick and accessible. They are priceless for wiping up after a run, washing your face when there's no water, and giving your pits a good swipe before hugging a new friend (old friends will understand). Be sure to check the ingredients of your baby wipes. Some include chemicals that smell nice, but don't agree with the dirtbag. Unscented is a must.

Where We Shower

If we're really itching for a hot, traditional, private shower, these are our options:

Campgrounds

Many state parks and even national parks that offer camping have public shower facilities. Some of these can be accessed by paying a day use fee or simply driving in. We have paid up to $5 to access a park with showers and drinking water. Some even offer sewage dumps. We have a national park pass, so sometimes we'll use the coin showers offered at parks like the Grand Canyon. It's $2 for about seven minutes, but it's a long seven minutes. I'll often be done before the time has run out, and I can just stand there letting the hot water run down my back.

Truck Stops

Many truck stops like Flying J offer shower services for a fee, but you get an entire small bathroom to yourself. There is soap and shampoo available, and there's no time limit. Those truckers really know how to live it up.

Gyms

We don't currently pay for a gym membership, but I know many dirtbags do. In an urban setting, this is usually the best way to get full access to showers. In Scottsdale, Arizona I visited a gym shower with a friend's free pass that was nicer than any home I have ever lived in.

Chapter 8: How To Clean

You probably know the drill of coming home after a long day of work, having to make dinner, then clean up after dinner, then do the dishes, then tidy up the rest of the house. By the time you've finished all your cleaning, the day is over and you're exhausted. You crash into bed, maybe read a little, then do it all again the next day.

Now imagine if you could clean your entire house in only ten minutes. Imagine if you could do a major spring clean in one hour. That's my current life. I cherish every minute I don't spend cleaning, because that always felt like wasted time to me. Now I can do it quickly and efficiently and it doesn't take up half my day.

By far the best strategy is to clean as you go. As soon as you're done using something, put it away. Do that dish immediately. Fold that sweater right away. Keep flat surfaces clear by tidying up daily. File work things away when you're done working, and minimize the effort you need to put into this.

Laundry

We do laundry once a month or less, and

sometimes I find only two or three clothing items from Shacky in there. His standards are set to slightly lower than mine, plus neither of us own many clothes. In all honesty, if it weren't for the animals we'd probably only need to do laundry once every three months. The majority of our washing involves blankets or towels the animals have puked on or soiled with accidental old-lady piddles from a dog who wishes to remain anonymous.

If we have water access via a creek or lake, we can take care of most of our laundry ourselves. After a run or workout, we'll take off our clothes, soak them in the stream (no soap), scrub them a little, then hang then up to dry. This takes care of the large majority of dirty clothes and we've done it several times.

Neither Shacky nor I wear underwear, so that reduces laundry. There is nothing we wear that we have to wash every single day. In fact, we prefer to wear as little as we can get away with, often shedding everything when we can get a sunny and remote spot. Plenty of sun and water on your body will keep you cleaner than an office job.

Good laundromats offer free wifi, are relatively clean, and don't force you to buy a charge card to do your laundry (instead of coins). The charge cards are useless for us since we are not likely to ever return to that location. We have purchased some to our loss, but normally we try to negotiate and trade coins for the use of someone else's card, explaining our passing-through situation. People seem open to this.

Sewage

We don't pay to dump sewage. Across the country you can find a variety of free sewage dumps, ranging from public parks to sewage treatment plants. We use an app called Sanidumps that helps us locate them.

If we're camping in a spot with a toilet, we can last more than two weeks before we have to dump sewage. If not, we prefer to dump once a week since hot temperatures can sometimes make the tank smell before it's completely full.

Our RV toilet is currently the greatest luxury we have. Without it, we'd spend a lot more time digging holes in the woods.

Chapter 9: Road-Friendly Travel Apps

For the first year of travel, we didn't have a cell phone. This was wonderfully liberating, but when we took on the challenge of crewing runners across the USA, we needed a way to communicate with them. We got a cheap pay-as-you-go deal at Walmart and soon grew dependent on some amazing apps. Here's what we used:

Gas Buddy

This app tracks and reports gas prices within a 50-mile radius. There is nothing more stressful than driving on an empty tank. We have had several scares where we couldn't find a gas station when we desperately needed one. If you are one of those people who try to push their gas to the last limits: change.

The Weather Channel

We rely heavily on weather reports to influence our choices of where to camp. In the past we have made the mistake of underestimating the weather. Winds and rain are major drawbacks, but hot temps are also a fine line due to the animals. Too hot, and we better find a camping spot with shade. Too cold, and we better make sure we have enough propane to run the heater.

Yelp

Yelp helps us find everything from coffee shops to oil change shops to vet clinics to breweries. Preferable to our RV Garmin, it's far more accurate and includes reviews. We rely on it heavily for any in-town chores.

Glympse

This app allows you to send someone your exact GPS coordinates and continues tracking you for up to four hours. Think of it as a very basic spot tracker. None of the places we camp have addresses and sometimes the directions can be complicated. This app allows our friends to find us.

WhatsApp

This is a free way to keep in touch with my friends and family in Canada. Canadian cell phone and text messaging plans are nowhere near where they should be in terms of access and affordability. International text messaging can really add up. With this app I can text my sisters, send photos, video, and even voice messages directly to them without being glued to Facebook.

Chapter 10: How To Travel With Pets

When you travel with pets, you have to be willing to do for them what most pet owners will never have to do for their animals. They are a priority before your own needs for comfort and adventure. They will slow you down, they will cancel your plans, they will drain your bank account, they will inconvenience you. And you have to be okay with that.

If you love a pet, you know that this is all worth it in the end. If it doesn't sound worth it to you, please don't travel with an animal. While a house-raised pet can be an accessory, a traveling pet is hard work. It is people. It requires a deep attention and intuition to their needs.

Ginger Dog's Story

Ginger is our senior pointer. My husband Shacky adopted Ginger as a tiny ball of white fuzz in 2003. Her litter had been abandoned in the streets of Tiajuana, Mexico, and she was brought to a halfway house in San Diego, where my husband found her.

Shacky was newly married at the time to his first wife and Ginger was an addition to that family. The marriage didn't last and soon it was just Ginger and Shacky. Shacky struggled with being a single doggie dad. His work and travel schedule were not conducive to owning a dog and Ginger spent many lonely hours home alone.

Shortly afterwards, I swept into the scene and threw my first ball for Miss Ginger. We've been besties ever since. We immediately started training for my first 100-mile race together and by the end of the year Ginger had free range of all beds and pillows and couches everywhere. I quickly lost interest in going anywhere or doing anything without her.

Ginger is easy to love. She is gentle and affectionate. The only things she longs for in this life is love and balls. When we bought the RV, Ginger hopped right in and refused to get out when we came home. She was ready for the road.

For the next two years, she lived a life most humans never get to experience. She saw the entirety of North America and sniffed everything from moose to salmon to porcupine. Her world view blew up.

Then in 2014, while chasing a ball, she slipped and fell and tore her CCL, a ligament in her knee. Our choices were to immobilize her almost completely for six months in a full-time crate, or fix it with surgery. Since I couldn't bear the thought of putting such an active dog in a crate for six months, we chose the least invasive surgery available. In retrospect, it was a mistake we would come to deeply regret.

The first surgery didn't take, so she had another. The second surgeon failed to remove the old hardware and this created an abscess in her leg that would never heal. The abscess led to a highly resistant infection we battled for two years. The only permanent solution would be another surgery, but by this time she was too weak to go under the knife. She had developed arthritis and incontinence. She started sleeping a lot more and our travel slowed considerably for her comfort. We were sure it was her last year of life and I made my peace with that.

Then in late 2016 just as I was finishing this book, she simply started improving. She was old Ginger again, playing in ways she hadn't done since she was a puppy. We took her to two separate vets who told us she was now strong enough to undergo surgery one more time, to fix her leg once and for all. She had the offending hardware removed in 2017 and has been making steady improvements ever since. I got my best friend back.

Mama Kitty's Story

We were in the process of purchasing the RV when I first spotted Kitty. She was living under an abandoned car parked on our residential street. There were a few feral cats in the area, but she was the most local. She looked like a kitten: tiny, famished, incredibly skittish.

I began leaving food out for her after work, and soon she was waiting at our door at dinner time. It was weeks before I could get close enough to pet her. Slowly, I moved her food into the house and got her to come inside. We kept Ginger on a leash indoors for almost 30 days while she learned that Kitty was not for eating. Ginger never really agreed to this, but tolerated the cat out of love for us.

In a matter of weeks I realized that Kitty was pregnant. The way I came to realize this was because tiny kittens started coming out of her one day. I lost my mind and Shacky rushed back home from work.

We delayed our dirtbag life for a few more weeks until her babies were weened and we could find good homes for them. By the time we were ready to drive away permanently, Kitty was domesticated. I could have given her away with the rest of her kids, except... I couldn't. So we threw her in the RV, stuck a litter box in the back, and drove away.

Kitty took to dirtbag life like a fish in water. She immediately called shotgun and if anyone else dared to ride in the front passenger seat, she would force-sit on their lap. She'd stick her head out the front window like a dog and when we parked, she'd howl at the door to be let out.

Over the years kitty and I built some trust. She had free reign of both indoors and outdoors, but rarely ventured far. She came home when I called her… mostly. If I went on a hike and called her to follow, she'd trot along behind me. At night she would curl up on my chest and crush my lungs while I slept, inducing nightmares in which I could not breathe. I adored her.

In March of 2016 I noticed she wasn't eating as much. Then she started swaying and tipping over while trying to walk. Her eyes would roll to the back of her head and she'd lose control of her body. We immediately rushed her to the vet and discovered she had Feline Infectious Peritonitis (FIP). The vet explained that there was no cure and she was days away from death. We agreed that the most compassionate decision was to stop her suffering and put her down immediately. It came as a complete shock. One day she was fine and the next her little life was over.

I held her close and we cuddled until she was purring so deafeningly loud that the vet couldn't hear her heartbeat through the stethoscope. Then they put my sweet kitty to sleep in my arms.

I had her cremated and spread her ashes in an aspen grove near one of her favorite campsites in Colorado where we had planned to spend the summer with her. I conducted a short funeral service, with only myself and the aspens as witnesses. It was right and true and real.

That summer I hiked out to visit her every single day, a strenuous two-hour trek at elevation. I hiked so much that my legs changed shape and I learned to move as swiftly as she did over boulders and creeks. That aspen grove became a sacred place for me and my daily journey there, a pilgrimage.

I still feel her with me today, riding shotgun on my lap and pressing into my chest while I sleep. One night I dreamed I saw her, stalking freely in the wilds of the universe, surrounded by space and stars. She was huge, more like a wild cat than a house cat. Her eyes were a piercing bright emerald. I held out my hand to her and she sniffed my fingers indifferently like she always used to. A few weeks after that, I began to see mountain lions in real life. Although I keep my distance and follow wild cat protocol, my soul understands that Kitty is never far from me.

Pros of Pet Travel

The pros of traveling with pets are the pros of owning pets in general: affection, companionship, photo ops, and dressing them up for Halloween. Except when you're traveling full-time, those benefits are amplified a thousand fold. The company is constant and the affection is deep.

Within the first few months of traveling with my dog, I noticed a very definite and distinct change in her personality. Where she was once skittish, she showed confidence. Where she was once fearful, she showed courage. She grew more social towards strangers, more tolerant of children, and more appreciative of the outdoors.

Her trust and obedience doubled. She listened and obeyed more quickly, transitioning from leash-only to voice-commands. She slept better at night. And she became an extension of me, like a sixth sense or a third arm. Whereas before I was comfortable putting her in a kennel for any multi-day adventures, I began loathing the time we spent apart.

I don't want to spend too much time discussing pros like I'm trying to sell the idea. If I need to convince you to travel with an animal, you probably shouldn't. An animal is going to completely change your travel experience and it's going to be much harder than traveling with humans, or alone.

In my experience, people who travel happily with pets are the sort for whom leaving them behind is not an option. The sort who don't normally go places where their animals are not welcome. In other words, my people.

Cons of Pet Travel

1. Dogs are not allowed in most American National Parks

While Canadian National Parks welcome dogs, many American parks don't allow them on the trails. Making alternate plans for the dog is an inconvenience and an expense. The Grand Canyon has a doggie boarding facility within the park and Zion National Park has a Doggie Dude Ranch just outside the park's borders. Other than that, we usually have to leave Ginger in the RV and cut our adventures short, or take turns so one of us can stay with her.

2. Well-meaning humans can become over concerned.

Some people will spot a dog in your vehicle and think they have to break a window to set it free, not understanding that our little camper has much better temperature regulation than a car. In addition to extra windows, we have a strong fan that often keeps the inside of the RV much cooler than outdoors.

Part of me is glad there are people who worry about other people's pets, but when I've taken great pains for my dog's well-being, it's annoying to meet a person who assumes I would leave her unattended in a place she's not completely safe.

3. Visiting non-dog-friendly homes can be

uncomfortable.

Some people have dog-free homes. Others have a dogs-outside rule. Others have homes so beautiful they are extremely reluctant to let animals enter at all. Those have all been deal-breakers for us.

4. Good vet care is hard to find.

Most vets charge a consultation fee that can range anywhere from $30-50 when it's the first visit. We've had to pay this fee multiple times. We've been told by some vets that their license doesn't allow them to prescribe medications for pick-up over state lines. Since we don't live in the same state year-round, sometimes we have to drive for miles for the medication she needs.

Traveling with a pet is difficult. It's a constant responsibility and it is so much more work than owning a home with an animal in it. Everything you do and everywhere you go, your pet is affected. Traveling full-time with animals requires a very special, full-time kind of animal lover.

Chapter 11: How To Make Social Connections

Connecting with others on the road can be difficult. The transient nature of travel, especially when you're moving quickly, means you are rarely seeing the same people on a daily basis. Even the introverted among us can appreciate a sense of community, particularly a close-knit one. As much as I love my time in the woods, there's something valuable and right in the gathering of good friends.

With full-time travel, I've found that my friendships have deepened. Not only have I met a greater number of people by surface contact alone, I have also had the opportunity to invest more time into the friendships I already had. For an old soul like me, this is a much more satisfying level of social connection.

Here are some of my favorite ways to be around other people for meaningful social contact:

Sign up for a race.

My husband and I are both trail runners and hikers, but in a race setting we are much more focused on socializing than in competing. We go to races to see our friends, share some miles with them, and enjoy new company in the outdoors. It's by far my preferred way of socializing. On a single track trail, you can catch someone one-on-one and you're never in a big crowd (we avoid all races where you are). The venue is intimate yet spacious, so it's easy to move from one person to the next.

Speak to strangers.

You do not need to know someone for a long time to make a strong connection with them. I have listened to people share their deepest hopes and fears on a first encounter. Being the recipient is easy. Just listen.

Get a library card.

People don't always think of libraries as social places, but they can be. Many libraries host groups or talks or book clubs. You could even set up your own talk based on your travels or your profession. Offer some of your own services up to the community. If you have a book or product to market, these opportunities can help you connect with a new customer or client base. Talk to your local librarian about these possibilities. In my experience, libraries are usually eager to host talks and readings.

Shout out on social media.

Sometimes I'll post our location on Facebook and

ask, "Who's in the area and wants to come over?" We've had many of our friends "visit" our campground and hang out for the day. They are spread all across the country and often we don't realize how close they are.

Facebook has given us endless opportunities as far as places to stay and people to meet. We have the luxury of meeting most of our Facebook "friends" in person as we travel across North America. It's amazing how different the in-person contact is to the online encounter. From the wide open road I echo the words of Walt Whitman: "I have looked for equals and lovers, and found them ready for me in all lands."

Chapter 12: How To Manage Expenses

I define financial success as being in a position of not having to constantly worry about money. Full-time travel and minimalist living gave me that gift. Although I am making less money, our expenses are low. The secret is not to make more money, but to find a way to spend less, own less, and need less. I feel lucky when I realize that this is the exact life I would be living if I were a millionaire: complete freedom to pursue my interests and full-time travel.

Some people assume that we don't work, that we're lazy, or that we're on government assistance. None of these assumptions are true. More than any other time in my life, I feel engaged and empowered and a part of a greater cause.

We very rarely spend more than $2,000/month. When Shacky is fishing for our food, it's closer to $1,000. This includes medical expenses for our senior dog, which is currently our third biggest expense. Food and gas are our main expenses. We don't pay rent. No mortgage. No car payments. No debts. No amenities (we are solar powered). No children. No monthly payments of any kind. No worries. Before hitting the road, my husband and I were earning about $65,000/year. Now we cumulatively earn about $15,000/year. Most of the work we do is in exchange for food or shelter, not money.

Here are the steps to the path we followed for financial freedom:

1. Build a nest egg.

Before we hit the road, I sold a condo in Canada and Shacky had sold some stock from the biotech company he was employed at. We began with a nest egg of $20,000, which I expected would support us for a year. Combined with my meager book sales, this egg has lasted us almost five years.

Many people don't have $20,000 just laying around in property and stocks, but how long would it take to save $5,000? This is the bare minimum I would recommend for a nest egg.

Having a nest egg doesn't mean you rely on it fully or that you're not working at the same time. Think of it as a buffer. It represents a peace of mind for emergency situations. It gives you the freedom to be a little more picky with the jobs you take on instead of settling in desperation for anything you can find. Every little bit helps.

How do you go about building this nest when you're already living paycheck to paycheck? The answer is: through sacrifice, as much as you're willing to take on. Remember, it's temporary. It might take you six months or a year to save the amount you need. I recently read about one couple who took two and a half years to save $95,000 by extreme frugal living. Before that, they were living paycheck to paycheck. Afterwards, they took the next three years to travel the entire globe.

2. Pick a tax-free haven.

This involves changing your state residency to one with little or no income tax. It doesn't matter whether you are physically residing in that state—if you set up legal residency there, you are covered by their tax laws. The first step we took before hitting the road was to change our state residence to South Dakota and get new plates. In total, we have spent three days in South Dakota over the past three years. Other popular states include Alaska, Florida, Nevada, Tennessee, Texas, and Washington. The most popular among RVers is Texas, South Dakota, and Florida.

All of these states have wonderful services available for travelers like us, such as mail forwarding services and assistance with driver's licenses, vehicle registration, voting, and insurance. We use a company called My South Dakota Address to receive mail and renew our vehicle registration without having to personally travel to South Dakota.

3. Slash expenses.

To maintain this lifestyle long-term without earning a steady income, you're going to need to keep expenses to a bare minimum. Our major expenses on the road are food and gas. We don't pay for any amenities. That doesn't mean we don't use amenities occasionally, just that we don't pay for them. Bartering and trading is almost always an option.

The easiest way to do this is to keep track of all your expenses in one month, then examine them closely. Which ones can you do without? Start with those. Which ones can you acquire without spending money? Try those too. In another month, revisit. I'm confident that after one month on the road you will have learned that you can actually get by with much less than you thought you needed.

Remember, by refusing to spend on the items that are less important to you, you are more free in the areas that do matter to you. The idea isn't to be frugal for the sake of frugality, but to focus your resources on the things that hold value for you personally.

4. Consider work for stay.

For most people, food and lodging are major monthly expenses. If you can figure out a way to exchange work for either, that's a win. Work for stay options are listed on websites like Workaday, HelpX, and WWOOF. This is also a great way to develop skills and educate yourself on farming and sustainable living. Workcamping jobs in exchange for lodging and amenities can also be researched on workamper.com and coolworks.com.

You normally work for 3-5 hours a day, then have the rest of the day to yourself. There is much more social contact as you are generally interacting with a family or fellow workers.

Artist-in-Residence programs (AiR) are another way to secure free lodging. TransArtists has the most complete database of AiR programs around the world. In these situations, you are fully sponsored to pursue your art full-time. You are given space and lodging to express your creativity on your own terms while your living expenses are covered. Most programs require a clear plan for what you are specifically planning to work on.

5. Choose your bank carefully.

Charles Schwabb is generally considered the best bank for full-time travelers. They reimburse all ATM fees, even international ones. We have had an account for years.

We have also kept smaller accounts with Union Bank and Wells Fargo based on where we are physically staying. For Canadian travelers, PC Financial seems to be your best Schwabb-equivalent with no bank fees.

Whatever bank you go with, make sure they have paperless options and/or a good app you can use on road. You'll want to automate everything as much as possible. I can't stress enough the importance of having a few different places to store money. Although Shacky and I share all our money, we have our own bank accounts. A few times we have been in situations where one of us can't access our accounts and the other has covered all expenses.

6. Cash is your best friend.

No matter how great your bank is, if you're not carrying a small amount of cash with you, you run the risk of being financially stranded at anytime. Since we don't normally camp in places that deliver mail, I have found myself in need of cash in situations where my bank card has been cancelled unexpectedly through no fault of my own. It can be weeks before I find myself in a location where I can receive a replacement card by mail. In the meantime, I can't access any of my money. I've learned the hard way to always keep a small nest egg of cash somewhere nearby for these types of emergencies.

7. Track expenses.

Full-time travel can feel like a long vacation, so it's tricky to keep track of expenses and stay on a budget, especially in the early years. We spared no expense during our first year of travel because we wanted to fully enjoy every "luxury" of being on the road. This amounted to a lot of eating out. Now we track our expenses and I am excited by the challenge of finding new ways to consume less and preserve our resources.

8. Don't forget to pay it forward.

Always take a little less than you need and always give a little more than you can afford. If there is any sure-fire recipe for adventure, it is simply that. Some call this faith and some call it generosity, but to me it is simply the only way I want to experience this life.

Chapter 13: How To Earn Money

There are endless ways to make money on the road, so it's really up to your skill set, your interest and your creativity. Our primary source of income is my book sales, including this one. If you purchased this book, thank you for supporting us.

I have friends who are supported by athletic sponsorships. Others who are associated with charities that help cover expenses. I know musicians who perform and compose music. We had our solar panels installed by a guy who lives off-the-grid in the middle of a desert in California and this is how he makes his living. Others rent out their homes for additional income.

One of our friends was working as a traveling carnival employee when we first met him. We have visited a holistic vet who works out of an RV. Others take months off at a time to work a "real job," saving up their money and hitting the road for the rest of the year.

When I think of all the options out there, I get excited. The Internet has transformed this lifestyle and the opportunities are overwhelming for aspiring dirtbags. Here are some of the major ones available in

Vanessa Runs

North America:

Seasonal Work

Park hosting is a go-to option for many in the RV community. You can host at a private RV park, a city or state park, a National Wildlife Refuge, or a National Forest campground. Hosting involves park maintenance for a few hours a day. Positions vary greatly. Those that involve customer service tend to pay better. Others don't pay at all. Hosts are generally set up with a free campground, free hookups, and water access. If you love the outdoors and love the idea of living at your favorite park for the season, this gig might suit you. You can check online for the options in your area.

Working on a boat is another seasonal option. The opportunities here depend on your skill and experience. Start in any position you can because it's fairly easy to acquire the skills you need on board and work your way up. Don't forget the larger yachts and cruise ships. Food and lodging is generally covered so most of your paycheck goes directly into your pocket. It's literally a free ride.

The sugar beet harvest is always looking for laborers in the fall. This job takes place in Montana, North Dakota, and Minnesota. It involves processing beets at a sugar factory. The jobs pay well and normally last three weeks. Most people make $3,000 -

$4,000 during that time. If you can drive a truck or operate a Bobcat, you can earn much more. Learn more at:

http://www.sugarbeetharvest.com/index.cfm?content=jobs

In December, Amazon distribution centers are hiring for the Christmas rush. These centers cater to campers, calling these employees the Camper Force. They pay well and provide a free campsite in an RV Park. The centers are generally located in rural areas and the work is labor-intensive. Learn more at: http://www.amazonfulfillmentcareers.com/opportunities/camper-force/

Speaking of Christmas, working at a Christmas tree lot can pay well and also offer free lodging. The same goes for pumpkin and firework lots. The options here vary greatly from town to town. Some Santa gigs are also surprisingly well paid, not to mention fun. Don't forget to look into tourist towns in general, especially during peak season. Many local businesses need to hire extra employees for the summer or winter rush.

If you're a nomadic poker dealer, you can make $10,000 in seven weeks by following poker tournaments across the country. These tournaments hire hundreds of dealers and the larger ones hire in the thousands. The perks are great and it's fairly easy to get trained and certified. You can learn more at: http://www.cheaprvliving.com/blog/nomadic-poker-dealer/

Digital Nomadism

The wiki definition of a digital nomad is an individual who uses telecommunication technologies to earn a living. Generally you are working remotely via wifi with a wide variety of employment options, many of them entrepreneurial. Some digital nomads share office spaces or use housesitting gigs as a home base. Others work out of their cars, RVs, coffee shops, etc.

Writing, online tutoring, and web design are common jobs. You'll also find voiceover artists, illustrators, coaches, and jewelry designers. It's impossible to generalize these jobs: anything goes as long as you can do it on the road. Freelance travel writing is probably the hardest market to break into. If you have a decent online following you may want to consider a sponsorship. We have one friend who rents out his teardrop trailer as advertising space for local businesses. He also receives free outdoor gear.

Keep in mind that you can freelance any skill or talent. You can cut hair. You can train dogs. You can even decorate and organize homes. Whatever skill you have, freelance it. Craigslist is a great place to pick up odd jobs, especially if you're in a larger city.

Lastly, consider attending an RV show for more job options. Many companies that attend these events hire dirtbags on the spot. Other resources for finding work on the road are:

- Guru
- Upwork
- Flexjobs
- Uber

Chapter 14: How To Stay Sustainable

This chapter is the closest to my heart.

A good guest pitches in around the house to help their host in gratitude for the hospitality. That's how I look at my time on this planet. I am a guest here, benefiting fully from the wide spectrum of joy that this blue-green orb has to offer. The very least I can do is leave as little a footprint as I can, and busy my hands with improving each new place I tread. To me this means consuming only the minimum I need to stay healthy and producing as little waste as possible.

I am so proud of the fact we have been able to drastically reduce our garbage, though I am still far from where I would like to be. Here is what I am currently doing to stay green on the road:

Buy in bulk.

We have a Costco membership that we use as much as possible for our staples. We visit bulk stores for rice, sardines, veggies, and potatoes. Occasionally we find discounts on whole birds like turkey or chicken. This greatly reduces the packaging we consume and saves us a lot of money. It also reduces the time we spend grocery shopping as one single haul can last for several months.

Buy local.

No matter how I break it down, it is always cheaper, healthier, most ethical and environmentally sustainable to buy local. We have enjoyed wild game in Alaska and fresh fish when we are near a water source. In small towns we eat as the locals do. In big cities we seek out weekly farmer's markets.

Go paperless.

Two years ago we banned paper towels from our humble home. We went out and purchased a bunch of rags to use instead, washing and reusing them. This transition was easier than I imagined. We also went paperless with mail and flyers. These days many banks and credit cards offer paperless options. We don't pick up junk mail or newspapers unless we are planning to use them for fire kindling.

Get a Kindle.

I am a book lover. When I first bought a Kindle, I was skeptical of how I would like digital books over physical ones. It turns out, I like digital books very much. And audiobooks too. The best part is that I have immediate, searchable access to all my books in any location.

Say NO to plastic.

The plastic we consume never disappears from this planet. Your plastic will outlive you. The best thing we can ultimately do is to stop producing it. The best tool I have to make that possible is to stop buying it. Every year I chip away at this goal in a more significant way.

Sign up for Zero Waste events.

I am part of a close-knit endurance community. Many of my friends register regularly for race events and spend hundreds of dollars a year on race registrations. I aspire to put my registration money to work. I learned that all Grand Circle Trail races are zero waste, in addition to boasting some of the most beautiful trails in the country. I have had the opportunity to learn and contribute to this zero waste strategy and I stand by it 100%. You can find seven spectacular and sustainable races at grandcircletrails.com.

Adopt a personal zero waste policy.

Don't be intimidated by this goal. It's a learning process and you won't get there in one day, but all of us can take small steps towards a more sustainable lifestyle. Make a personal commitment to reuse, recycle, or compost. It is no longer enough to pack out our garbage on a hike or poop in the woods. We must stop purchasing outdoor products that contribute to landfills. Look carefully at the fuels and gear you are using. Is your nutrition packaging recyclable? Will your fuel wrappers exist on this planet longer than you will?

Remember: Refuse, reduce, reuse, recycle, and rot. In that order. Now is the time to make this transition. Future generations are evolving to demand less, not more. It's not too late. I hope you'll join me in stepping gently into the future.

Chapter 15: How To Work Offline

When you have constant internet access it's hard to imagine a life that's primarily off-grid. I type up emails, read articles, write blog posts, and create social media posts all offline. When I get an internet connection, I press send.

One of the things that first excited me about being on the road was the thought that I would have unlimited time to work at my own pace. I would be my own boss and set my own hours. Well, it turns out I'm a pretty lenient boss. It took me about a year to learn that absolute freedom in the way of goals and deadlines is not easier, but harder.

I work well under pressure and I work best when I have a firm deadline. On the road, I struggled with getting things done in a timely manner. By the second year of travel, I had developed a system that worked efficiently for me. Here are my best tips for staying productive as a dirtbag.

1. Set up a mailing address.

The absolute easiest thing to do about mail, especially if you're not planning to permanently live on the road, is to have a family member or close friend agree to collect your mail. Your mother would be the obvious choice. You want to make sure it's someone you can trust and who can contact you if any important mail arrives.

My family is too far to receive my mail, so we pay for a mailing service with a company called My South Dakota address. For anything we order online, we generally solicit the help of a nearby friend.

2. Do one thing at a time.

Multitasking used to be an advantage in my cubicle life, but it's a nightmare in my dirtbag life. Although it doesn't feel like there's a lot going on, distractions are endless. You never really come to that place of routine and comfort, where you can tune out your daily surroundings. Most places are new places and most people are new people and you're always aware of them around you.

I make it a priority to focus on one task at a time, even when that task is as simple as feeding the dog. This also helps keep me present within my surroundings. I am not mindlessly going through my checklist, but really focused on each thing and doing it well.

3. Do things every day or not at all.

In a life where routine is so rare, I need this type of stability. Every task that is important to me, I do daily and in order of importance. My important tasks are not always work-related. Sometimes it's a long run or hike. Most often, it's writing.

4. Try the Pomodoro technique.

This technique works by setting a timer for 25 minutes, and working non-stop through that stretch of time. When the time expires, take a five-minute break. Then reset the timer to 25 minutes and get back to work. I like to do five rotations before taking a 30-minute break. If I am interrupted during the 25 minutes, I simply stop, regroup, and re-start the timer as soon as I can.

The idea behind this technique is to maximize productivity. The intermittent breaks, where I usually do something physical, go a long way to clear my mind and re-set my motivation for the next chunk of work time. I have a free Pomodoro app on my laptop that I run while I'm working. It automatically counts me down, beeps when it's break time, and re-starts.

5. Focus on creating content.

Not everything I create is a work of art every single day of the week, but working towards creating something new on a daily basis keeps me engaged in my work and stimulates my mind towards fresh ideas. One of my main goals is to create things of truth and beauty and relevance.

Chapter 16: How To Give And Accept Hospitality

Many don't know how to be good guests and great hosts. I think it's because we're out of practice. In a world where everyone has everything, hospitality is a lost art. Many of us travel with plenty of food and amenities, but when you put yourself in a place of need, even in a small way, you ignite in others a desire to share. Serving makes us feel good.

Receiving hospitality is harder than offering it. We all like to feel independent and self-sufficient, but the truth is that we need each other. It's hard to put yourself in a place of need, and even harder to ask for help. Give others a chance to give and always give freely yourself.

Here are my tips on how to accept hospitality graciously and be a great guest:

1. Don't overstay your welcome.

Most hosts will say, "Stay as long as you like," but of course... you shouldn't really. You need to be conscious and respectful of other people's space. Since I am so deeply protective of my own space, I get it. The easiest way to not overstay is to set a length of time for your visit. Maybe arrange a meet-up around a meal or an activity, then leave when it's over.

Sometimes these stays can be longer — say, you've been invited to stay for the season. If that's the case, and if you've been specifically invited for that amount of time, you still shouldn't get too comfortable. A length of stay more than 3-7 days means that you need to start contributing something. Your host is not your slave nor your mother.

2. Make yourself useful.

A true host will never ask you to complete any chores while in their home, but that doesn't mean you shouldn't. Many well-meaning guests make the mistake of asking their hosts if they need help. Don't ever ask — just start working like it's your job. Your host will refuse — that's courtesy. It's your job to persist. If your host is adamant in their refusal and it looks like it will break into a fist fight, you can give in. Otherwise, roll up your sleeves and show your gratitude in a real and practical way. Cleaning up after yourself is the absolute bare minimum you should be doing.

Chores are the easiest and usually best way to help. Be observant and make a mental note of all the chores your host is already doing. Then take over. Beat them to it, when they're not around to fight you. Have it done before they even get home.

The Dirtbag Handbook

If you're staying longer than three months, offer to pay rent. If they refuse, contribute to food and toiletries. If they refuse that, just buy whatever they need and put it away. Make sure you stay true to their regular brands. Don't replace their fancy-ply toilet paper that feels like feathers on your ass with some see-through rolls you stole from a portapotty.

Sometimes you'll encounter people who really like things done a certain way and would truly prefer that you not touch anything. But generally, these are not the people who invite guests to invade their homes for months at a time. Use your judgment. It's easy to tell if someone is happy or upset that you have done a chore for them. If they re-do all your work, it means you literally shouldn't have.

3. Always leave on a high note.

Remember that Seinfeld episode where George Constanza learns how much better he is received when he keeps leaving on a high note? He would disappear completely after making people laugh, and they were always left wanting more. Do that. Tell your best story and then say goodnight. If you can develop this skill, you'll very rarely be unwelcome.

4. Show interest in your hosts.

When someone invites you to their home, it's not a completely selfless act. Of course, it is nice and generous of them and you should be grateful, but you're not a charity. If they invite you over, it's because they are interested in you and you should be interested in them. If you find they are of absolute zero interest to you, don't go. If you're already there, don't stay long and don't come back. Both host and guest should get something from the visit.

Your hosts want to hear your stories. They want to know about your travels. They are interested in your tips, your likes, your dislikes, and most importantly: they want to share their own experiences. Ask questions. Look alive. Show some interest.

With the right people, this should come easily. If you find you are forcing yourself to show interest, move on until you find your tribe. Visiting is about sharing more than a home. It's about sharing your lives and experiences.

For online communities that connect you to strangers, like Couchsurfing.com, this is especially true. These strangers aren't inviting you in because you're good-looking. They want to hear where you've been and where you're going. They want to show off their town, suggest places for you to visit, and parade their favorite things for you to admire.

Make sure your time is flexible enough to visit their recommended places or eat at their favorite restaurants. Let them guide you through the best of their cities. Help with dinner. Bake a cake together. Start a board game. Complete a puzzle. With strangers, it's about getting to know the other person. If that sounds torturous to you, don't accept the hospitality.

It's worth noting that you don't need to be an extrovert to do these things. If you're a dirtbag, chances are you're fascinated by life. And if you're fascinated by life, you're fascinated by people. This is what travel is all about. Exposure. Expose yourself to everything you possible can. Let your curiosity rage. Ask questions, get to know your hosts, see life through their eyes. You'll both be better for it.

5. Bring a gift.

This is one of those "rules" that seems antiquated, but I still like to practice it if I can. The fact that it's not always expected is actually a plus: when I actually do it, it looks and feels really good. I'm the type of person who loves giving things away, but when you're a full-time dirtbag it's a bit of a creative challenge since you don't travel with much.

Sometimes it's truly the thought that counts. No one is expecting an expensive gift. Do something creative instead, especially if you can make it yourself. If you have kids, have them make a card. I usually give my books away. If you don't have a gift, then gift your services for something specific, like babysitting or petsitting. The point is, do or bring something that lets your host know you appreciate and care for them.

6. Eat what is offered.

In the past we have followed fairly strict diets on the road: vegan, paleo, high fat, fruitarian, you name it. However, when we visit someone in their home and share a meal with them, we'll eat anything. This is important to me: eating what my host eats, and not making them go out of their way to prepare a special meal. This is about community, not food. We have eaten some great, healthy meals and we have eaten some terribly unhealthy ones. But you clean your plate and be grateful for it, just like your mama said. Everyone who is serving you is doing their best.

7. Know when to say no.

Sometimes the kindest thing you can do is refuse an invitation. We get a lot of invitations and if we wanted to, we could visit a home almost daily. But that's not the lifestyle I want. I'm also on the introverted side and although I love visiting people, if I do it too often I'll burn out. It's never fair to expose an unsuspecting host to your grumpy side because you said yes when you wanted to say no. When I feel I have nothing more to offer, I'll take a raincheck. My priority is myself and I need to manage my own energy.

The Dirtbag Handbook

How to Host a Dirtbag

Are you passionate about supporting your local dirtbags, but aren't sure what exactly they need (other than a shower, obviously)? For you, I have compiled this handy list of what your dirtbag needs but may be too polite to ask for.

1. Shower

Let's start with the glaringly obvious. The two things your dirtbag will appreciate the most: a little privacy and hot water. When you're used to freezing creeks and public nudity, a hot shower is like bathing in a unicorn's tears of joy.

2. Laundry facilities

There is only one thing that stinks worse than a dirtbag: their dirtbag of laundry. Keep in mind: these were clothes that were rejected by the dirtbag as being too dirty on their scale of extremely low standards. If you are fortunate enough to have a washer and dryer in your home, do the universe a favor and lend them out to the dirtbag cause. CAUTION: Do NOT attempt to load the washer for your dirtbag. They have been training for months to withstand the force of this smell.

3. Home-cooked meal

This doesn't have to be the least bit fancy or even all that good. Oops—did the salt slip? Did you use the wrong spice? It's already better than your dirtbag's last meal of cold Poptarts and tears.

4. Leftovers

This can be as simple as a sandwich or as easy as that old lasagna that's been sitting in the back of your fridge for three weeks. A dirtbag will respond with enthusiastic glee. Legend has it that some dirtbags have even been offered to-go beer, otherwise known as Dirtbag Nirvana.

Remember: Dirtbags can be shy and solitary creatures, but with only a few friendly offers you may easily find yourself with a new (or slightly used) dirtbag friend for life.

Chapter 17: The Things I Have Learned

While tourism is about seeing new sights, dirtbag life is about seeing the world with new eyes. In the years I have spent on the road, there is hardly one thing I have not changed my mind about. Here are some of the things I have learned:

I used to think the secret to success was not caring what others thought of me. I was wrong. The secret to my success lies in not trying to change my true nature because of what others think, in not being defined by what others think, and in not feeling shame because of what others think. But I must care. Caring is my only link to empathy and compassion and connection.

I have learned to travel deeply, not just widely.

I have learned to embrace foolishness, but never ignorance.

I have learned that dogs are human and cats are human and trees are human and even people are human. We are all life and life is always precious. We are not just connected; we are actually the same. A sin against my brother is a sin against myself. I no longer look at my brother who is different and think, "We are equals!" I look at him and say, "You are Me. And I am

You. And We are Here."

I have learned that I don't need everyone to like me. I don't need to win them over or convince them that what I'm doing is right for me. I need to allow people to feel hatred for me without feeling pressure to justify my choices.

I have learned that I don't need to own something in order to love it.

I have learned that I am too hard on others when I am too hard on myself. When I am angry that others aren't living up to my expectations, it's only because I am ungentle with myself. I can't accept the world as it is until I can accept myself for who I am.

I have learned to ask for what I need, not with hints or suggestions or riddles or body language, but with my God-given voice. I have learned that just because I need something doesn't mean I have to pay for it.

I have learned to dream without financial limitations. I have learned to nurture, protect, and grow my dreams into reality.

I have learned that I never need an excuse for a nap.

I have learned that I am magic. Anything I wish for, my faith can make it so. At anytime, I can change my life. I can disappear completely, just because it pleases me. Then appear again, soul transformed, with a cackle and a song.

I have learned to put myself in the way of pain and walk gladly the path of suffering. I have learned to bear witness to the struggles of my species and my non-species with eyes wide open and heart unshielded.

I have learned it's okay to cry.

I have learned to heal and re-heal myself with music and animals.

I have learned I don't need to be shy or embarrassed about my light. I don't need to hide or downplay my strength to make others comfortable. I don't need to pretend to be dumber, smaller, less excited, less emotional than I really am just to make friends.

I have learned that nothingness is not boring. Only boring people get bored.

I have learned to take notice of how my body moves on this planet. How hard my lungs are working, how my muscles ache, how hungry or thirsty I am under what conditions. I have learned to become an expert on myself. To become my own advocate, my own protector, my own muse, my own healer, and most passionately — my own biggest fan.

I have learned that time is more precious than money. I will not waste one second doing something I don't really want to, not even for pay. This doesn't mean I don't do hard things. It means I only do the hard things I want to do.

I have learned to use the following phrases to slow down my world long enough to understand it: "I need more time. No, thank you. I'm not ready yet. Not right now. I'm not finished with that. Please come back later. That's not my nature. Thank you for your patience."

I used to tread the same trails over and over again like a pilgrimage, believing these lands to be holy. When I was away from this wilderness, I would feel my soul wither and harden into a little black seed. In a panic I would claw my way back to the hills. Then I learned that it wasn't the land itself that was holy, but my feet that were divine. I learned to hold the immense wilderness in my own little heart. Now I can commune with the mountains while I'm standing in line. I can swim with the salmon while stuck in traffic. It is not the soft soil that is holy, mijitos. We are the holy ones.

I have learned that if I treat time like a bandit, it will behave like one and flee from me. I treat it instead like an old friend, with affection and ease. I hold my minutes loosely and they settle by my side. My days swell. My mornings drag. My sunsets linger. Until I grow impatient and set my gaze on the next adventure under this rambling sky.

See you there.

Afterword

"Once in a while it really hits people that they don't have to experience the world in the way they have been told to."
– Alan Keightley

Now forget everything I've written.

There are countless how-to-travel books that will tell you exactly what to do, where to go, and what to avoid. The real journey is yours. Your story is yet to be written. Don't let too much research rob you of this experience.

Dirtbag life is about going your own way and making your own mistakes. It's about learning on your feet and exploring your interests. Nobody can make a travel plan for you more perfect than the one you can build for yourself. Half the adventure is figuring it out in the moment.

Yes, there will be insecurity and uncertainty. Yes, you will make costly mistakes. I have too. So what? You figure it out. You ask for help. You learn quickly.

Our time on this planet is so short. Don't wait to see all the things. Don't wait to be your best self. Don't wait to stumble after the things that bring you joy. That is your right. Don't be afraid to break a little skin — this body regenerates.

Travel according to your favorite weather. Travel according to your interests. Travel according to the skills you want to acquire. See the major places. See the minor places. See the places everyone has been. See the places when no one goes. And go, because you want to. Then buckle in for a wild ride.

If you are reading these words, I hope you will do me the honor of joining my virtual tribe. This is a monthly letter of updates I send to those who have opted in. You can opt in at vanessaruns.com.

If you enjoyed this book, please consider leaving an Amazon review. If you purchased a hard copy of this book, please consider donating it to your local library when you are finished reading it. Until then, tread gently mijitos. Don't forget to compost.

About the Author

Vanessa and her husband Shacky continue to travel in their Rialta with dog in tow (Kitty went to heaven or hell during the time I was writing this book). You can follow their adventures at vanessaruns.com or read more about Vanessa's transition to dirtbag life in her memoir, The Summit Seeker: Memoirs of a Trail-Running Nomad. Vanessa's second book, Daughters of Distance: Stories of Women in Endurance Sports, is further inspiration. You can follow Vanessa on

Facebook at fb/vanessaruns or Twitter and Instagram @vanessaruns.

Acknowledgements

A sincere thank you to my long-suffering publisher, Ray Charbonneau at Y42K Publishing. He is also responsible for the book cover.

Thanks to Luis Escobar for the back cover photo.

Thank you to my tribe for your ongoing support.

Thank you to my sisters, all five of them, for bringing out my best self.

Thank you to Kitty for making me wild. And thank you to all the kitties on this planet who still find me in the canyons.

Made in the USA
Middletown, DE
14 September 2019